Kate and Gail

Suzanne I. Barchers

Consultants

Robert C. Calfee, Ph.D.
Stanford University

P. David Pearson, Ph.D.
University of California, Berkeley

Publishing Credits

Dona Herweck Rice, *Editor-in-Chief*
Lee Aucoin, *Creative Director*
Sharon Coan, M.S.Ed., *Project Manager*
Jamey Acosta, *Editor*
Robin Erickson, *Designer*
Cathie Lowmiller, *Illustrator*
Robin Demougeot, *Associate Art Director*
Heather Marr, *Copy Editor*
Rachelle Cracchiolo, M.S.Ed., *Publisher*

Teacher Created Materials

5301 Oceanus Drive
Huntington Beach, CA 92649-1030
http://www.tcmpub.com

ISBN 978-1-4333-2907-4

© 2012 by Teacher Created Materials, Inc.

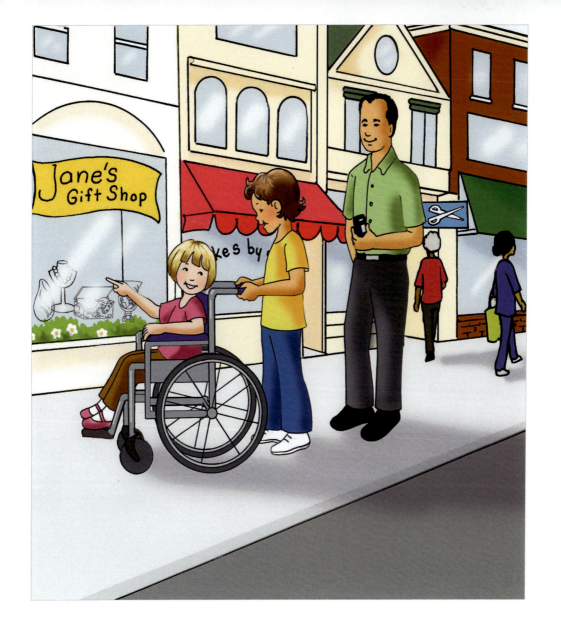

Dad takes Kate and Gail to Main Street.

Kate and Gail see some lace in a case.

Kate and Gail see a face on a vase.

Kate and Gail see a cake that Jake made.

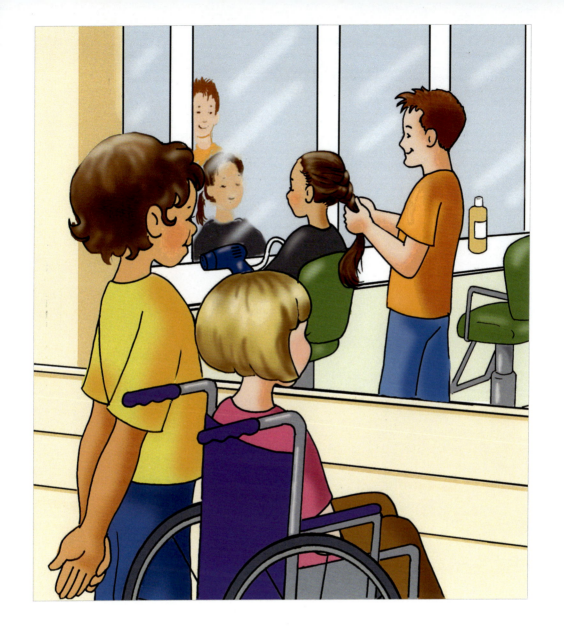

Kate and Gail see Gabe make a braid.

Kate and Gail see nails in a pail.

Kate and Gail see Dale with the mail.

Kate and Gail see an ape in a cape.

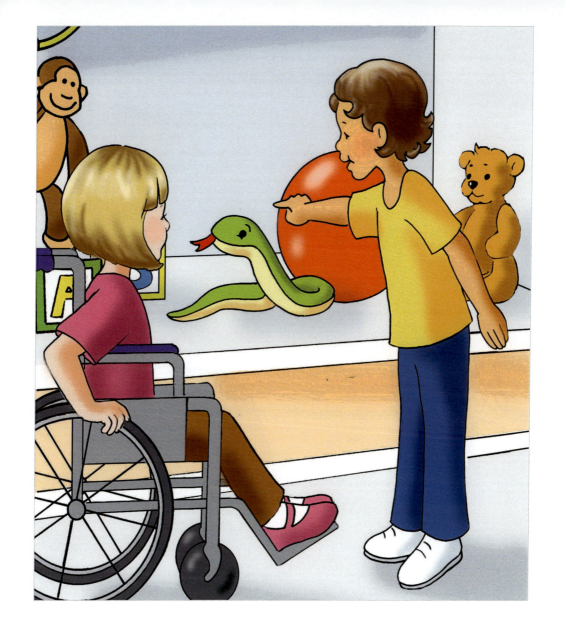

Kate and Gail see a snake that is fake.

Kate and Gail see grapes on a plate.

Kate and Gail see dates in a crate.

Kate takes Gail to her gate. Main Street is first-rate!

Decodable Words

an	face	mail
and	fake	Main
ape	Gabe	make
braid	Gail	nails
cake	gate	on
cape	grapes	pail
case	in	plate
crate	Jake	snake
Dad	Kate	takes
Dale	lace	vase
dates	made	

Sight Words

a	that
her	the
is	to
see	with
some	

Challenge Words

first-rate
street

Extension Activities

Discussion Questions

- Why do you think Kate and Gail go for a walk on Main Street?
- Who are some of the people Kate and Gail see? (*Dale and Gabe*)
- Which business would you like to visit? Why?
- Why do you think Main Street is called first-rate?

Exploring the Story

- Talk about the words *case*, *face*, and *lace*. Write them so you can see how they are spelled. Notice that they all end with a silent *e*. Discuss how the words all have the long *a* vowel sound. Then, write the words *Gail*, *mail*, and *pail*. Ask how these words are different from *case*, *face*, and *lace*. Discuss how the letter combination *ai* also makes the long *a* vowel sound.
- Look around and identify words that have the long *a* vowel sound. Make a list of the words on a sheet of paper. (Possible words include *drain*, *drape*, *frame*, *game*, *page*, *pane*, *rake*, *scale*, *skate*, *stake*, and *tape*.)
- Take a walk along a street that has a variety of businesses. Read the signs on the storefronts. Some will be informative, such as *Main Street Hardware*. Some will be cute, such as *Main Street Manes*. Some might rhyme, such as *Cakes by Jake*. Make a list of your favorite names. Discuss why they are favorites. Brainstorm new names for businesses.